Charles Ogilvie

On subscription to the Thirty-nine articles

As by law required of candidates for holy orders and of the clergy

Charles Ogilvie

On subscription to the Thirty-nine articles
As by law required of candidates for holy orders and of the clergy

ISBN/EAN: 9783337282813

Printed in Europe, USA, Canada, Australia, Japan

Cover: Foto ©Suzi / pixelio.de

More available books at **www.hansebooks.com**

ON

SUBSCRIPTION

TO

THE THIRTY-NINE ARTICLES

AS BY LAW REQUIRED

OF

CANDIDATES FOR HOLY ORDERS

AND OF

THE CLERGY.

BY

CHARLES A. OGILVIE, D.D.

REGIUS PROFESSOR OF PASTORAL THEOLOGY, AND CANON OF
CHRIST CHURCH, OXFORD.

———

OXFORD,
JOHN HENRY AND JAMES PARKER;
AND 377, STRAND, LONDON.
1863.

ADVERTISEMENT.

In putting forth the following Pamphlet, the Author desires to state that the consideration of the subject, to which it refers, so belongs to his own department of Academical duty as, in his judgment, to render proper and even necessary, at the present crisis, an avowal of his views and sentiments through the Press.

He regrets that, under the existing circumstances of the University of Oxford and of the Church, a controversial character has been unavoidably imparted to his Remarks.

CHRIST CHURCH, OXFORD,
    Oct. 30, 1863.

'

ON

SUBSCRIPTION,

&c.

A RECENT recommendation to "remove the
" existing Subscriptions" of the Church of England,
" as mischievous and useless[a]," undoubtedly de-
rives some importance from the authority, now
partly seen and partly surmised to lend a sanction
to it. The fact of such sanction can no longer be
denied and is to be deeply lamented, as an occasion
of "much grief" for many, compelled reluctantly
to acknowledge that a cause, of which they
earnestly deprecate the success, is espoused " by
" men, whom God hath endued with graces both
" of wit and learning for better purposes[b]."

It is however obvious that the authority in
question is unduly magnified and greatly exag-
gerated by the eager desires of the lovers of
change, on the one hand, and by the fears of
those, who dread lest Innovation should lead to
Revolution, on the other. The bold announcement
of (so called) Reform, which has been lately heard,
may have startled some, who are astonished at

[a] A Letter to the Lord Bishop of London, by Arthur
Penrhyn Stanley, D.D. &c. &c. p. 54.

[b] Hooker's Eccles. Pol. v. 41, 4.

B

discovering that a measure, strange to their ears, is openly avowed, zealously advocated and plausibly defended by a " Theological Professor in the " great University of Oxford and an Examining " Chaplain in the Diocese^c" of the Bishop, to whom he addresses an urgent appeal and by whom he evidently expects that appeal to be accepted with favour. But the proposal can have caused neither surprise nor alarm to well-informed and considerate persons. They are aware that it is not now for the first time brought forward. They have no difficulty in tracing its renewal, in the present day, to combined circumstances, Political, Ecclesiastical and Academical, which are at length deemed propitious to a full disclosure and even to an adoption of plans and schemes, that ·have long been regarded with approval in certain quarters. The late Dr. Arnold—who is never to be mentioned, even by such as have most widely differed from him, without the respect due to eminent abilities and acquirements, as well as to uncommon elevation and energy of moral character— some years ago contended for " a relaxation of " the terms of Subscription, and for a total repeal " of the 36th Canon ;" and, by " a relaxation of " the terms of Subscription," he explained himself to mean, that " the promise to use the Liturgy " should be the peculiar Subscription of the " Clergy and that the Articles should stand as

c Letter, &c. p. 3.

" Articles of peace, in the main draft of each
" Article, for Clergy and Laity alike[d]." His dis-
ciples and followers have diligently employed the
interval of upwards of twenty years since his death
in imbuing the minds of all within reach of their
influence with his and their sentiments, on this and
on every kindred subject. They have succeeded to
a considerable extent and appear to be sanguine in
the hope of accomplishing an object, like that
which the Feathers' Tavern Petitioners to the
House of Commons of the last Century, and certain
Petitioners to the House of Lords of the present
Century, had at heart, but were unable to effect.

Of each of these two attempts a brief notice may
be suitably taken here.

On the 6th of February, 1772, a Motion was made
in the House of Commons that a Petition, signed by
about 300 persons[e], Clerical and Lay, and called
the Feathers' Tavern Petition, from the place where
its originators and supporters had met, be brought
up. The Prayer of the Petition was, for " relief
" from such an imposition upon the judgment of

[d] Life of Dr. Arnold, vol. ii. pp. 179, 180.

[e] The chief promoters of the design and of an Association,
which had formed and matured it, were Archdeacon Blackburne; Rev. Theophilus Lindsey, who had married the Archdeacon's step-daughter; Rev. Dr. Disney, who married the
Archdeacon's own daughter; and Rev. Dr. John Jebb. The
three latter all resigned their Preferments and withdrew
from the Ministry of the Church, after 1772.

" the Petitioners as the laws relating to Subscription,"
were by them felt to lay; and for " restoration" to
what they considered their " undoubted right as
" Prostestants of interpreting Scripture for them-
" selves, without being bound by any human
" explications thereof, or required to acknowledge,
" by Subscription or Declaration, the truth of any
" Formulary of religious faith and doctrine what-
" soever, beside Holy Scripture itself." Sir Roger
Newdegate (then one of the Burgesses for the
University of Oxford, as he was from 1751 to 1780)
opposed the Motion, which, on a Division, was
negatived, by 217 against 71. Mr. Burke took
part in the Debate and voted in the majority.

On the 26th of May, 1840, a Petition, which
Dr. Arnold had signed, was presented in the
House of Lords; and its Prayer " that the letter
" of the Prayer Book and the Subscription to the
" Articles and Liturgy, might be rendered consist-
" ent with the practice of the Clergy and the ac-
" knowledged meaning of the Church," was warmly
supported by Dr. Stanley, then Bishop of Norwich,
and as warmly opposed by Dr. Blomfield, then
Bishop of London.

It seems to be in the confident expectation of a
better success that an attempt of the same sort
is now once more made. Unfortunately, however,
for the fulfilment of such expectation, no fresh
argument in favour of a formerly entertained
but defeated project has been stated; and, since

none has been stated, it is to be presumed that none has been discovered. They, who have been at the pains to sift and examine the mass of materials, which preceding controversies on the subject have accumulated, will meet with nothing new, in the way of reasoning, on the present occasion. They will only have to reflect that a subject, in its own nature somewhat dry and uninteresting, has been adapted to modern taste by the skilful handling of a popular writer. They will observe that, as before, so now, reflections are cast, sometimes openly, but oftener by implication, on a large body of the existing Clergy, as liable to charges of insincerity and prevarication, and on the long succession of wise and good men, who have cheerfully subscribed to the Articles in times past and have been utterly unconscious of the pressure of a burden that is become intolerable to the quickened sagacity, forsooth, and the keen moral perception, of these later days! If reflections and imputations of this sort were hailed with welcome in a former generation, it was because they indicated the existence within the Church and even within the inclosure of the Ministry of the Church, of a certain amount of sympathy with the declared enemies of the Constitution of England, in both Church and State, seriously threatened some time before, as well as at and after, the perilous crisis of the French Revolution. Among the most conspicuous of those enemies, denounced by Mr. Burke, were Richard Price and Joseph Priestley. The former, on whom the University of Aberdeen conferred the degree of D.D. in 1769, was a Dissenting Minister, well known in his day for writings on Political Economy and similar subjects. He was the friend and ally of Priestley, who received the Degree of LL.D. from the University of Edinburgh ; and who during seven years, i. e. from 1773 to 1780, was closely connected with the family of the Earl of Shelburne, afterwards first Marquis of Lansdowne, and father of that "illustrious Marquis," of whom we have been lately told that he was "dissuaded from coming to Oxford," in early life, "on the ground that it was a nest of "perjury'." Whatever else Oxford might at that time have been, it was not likely to be the place chosen for the education of his son by a Nobleman, whose companion and librarian had been one, who became the avowed advocate of the Materiality of the Soul, of the doctrine of Necessity and of Unitarianism ; and who, although he seems to have alienated his Patron by the advance of his opinions and his bold acknowledgment of such advance, claimed and to the day of his death continued to receive a handsome pension from that Patron.

Priestley's adherence to the cause of the French Revolution gained for him a nomination to

' Letter, &c. p. 24.

citizenship of the Republic, but involved him in serious trouble at Birmingham, where he was for some years the Minister of a Dissenting congregation. He was invited to succeed* his friend Dr. Price, whose death left vacant a place at Hackney; but, soon finding or fancying himself the object of general suspicion and enmity at home, went into voluntary exile in America and died there in 1804. His reputation for Chemical and Scientific discoveries has not shielded his name and memory from that withering exposure of his flagrant errors and his shallow pretensions to scholarship, to an acquaintance with the history of the early Church and to Theological learning, which is conveyed through a volume of Tracts in controversy with him[g]. This notorious Heresiarch and Democrat thought proper to step forward and meddle in the controversy, to which the publication of the Confessional[h] gave rise. He professed to

[g] The Title of this Volume, which will ever retain its value for the Student of Theology, is as follows:

" Tracts in controversy with Dr. Priestley, upon the His-
" torical Question of the Belief of the First Ages in our
" Lord's Divinity. Originally published in the years 1783,
" 1784 and 1786. Now revised and augmented with a large
" addition of Notes and Supplemental Disquisitions by the
" Author, Samuel, Lord Bishop of St. David's." 8vo. 1789.

[h] " The Confessional, or a Full and Free Inquiry into the
" right, utility and success of establishing Confessions of Faith
" and Doctrine in Protestant Churches," was composed some years before but was first published in 1766, without the

defend Archdeacon Blackburne, the author of
that work, and his associates, on the ground that,
in his opinion, " the most scrupulous casuist might
" allow a Clergyman, who is dissatisfied with the
" Church, to make a fair attempt to procure the
" reformation of those abuses that are intolerable
" to him ; and consequently to wait a proper time,
" to see the effect of his endeavours, before he
" absolutely quitted his station in the Church[i]."
But he could not conceal—he could ill disguise—
the estimate, which he and others had formed
of those, whom they affected to applaud, whilst he
spoke of " the anguish of that man's mind, who,
" if he *can* reconcile himself to continuing in a
" situation, into which he has introduced himself
" by a Subscription, which nothing could induce
" him to repeat, is yet obliged (if he officiate as a

Author's name. A second edition appeared in 1767, and a third,
corrected and enlarged, in 1770. As soon as it was known
that the Author of this work was Francis Blackburne, In-
cumbent of Richmond, Yorkshire, and Archdeacon of Cleve-
land, it was naturally expected that he would resign his
preferment and withdraw from the Ministry of the Church ;
but, to the surprise and disappointment of many, he declined
the offer of a congregation of Dissenters in London, who
desired to have him for their Minister and continued to the
day of his death, in the year 1787, to retain the places that
had been accepted and were held on the condition of a
Subscription, which he declared himself utterly unable to
renew.

[i] Dr. Priestley's Considerations on Church Authority,
p. 83.

" Clergyman at all) solemnly to recite sentiments,
" which he believes to be absurd, if not absolutely
" impious[k]."

Warmed with his theme and apparently forgetful of the false position, in which he had placed
himself, as a vindicator of certain Clergymen whom
he praised, he proceeded to inquire : " What must
" people think, to see those, who are appointed
" to instruct them in the principles of religion
" and morality, solemnly subscribing to Articles of
" Faith, which they are known to disbelieve and
" abhor ? And who among the Clergy, that read
" and think at all, are supposed to believe one
" third of the Thirty-nine Articles of the Church
" of England[l] ?"

It is in the same spirit, it is with the same
outward show of approbation, and the same half-
suppressed yet cutting censure, that the leaders of
the Political Dissenters of our own day bestow
their fulsome commendations on Divinity Pro-
fessors and Bishops, whom they are pleased to call
liberal and whom they perceive to be serviceable
for the promotion of their ends—ends, which they
are too prudent unnecessarily to declare, but which
they do not hesitate, on suitable occasions, to
avow. " The total demolition of the Polity of
" his country in the Ecclesiastical branch[m] " was the

---

[k] Considerations, &c. p. xi. of Preface.

[l] Considerations, &c. p. 59.

[m] Tracts in controversy with Dr. Priestley, &c. p. 402.

object at which Dr. Priestley sometimes frankly confessed that all his endeavours from the press and from the pulpit aimed. At the very same object our Political Dissenters aim ; and a candid acknowledgment that they do so has either escaped them, when they have been off their guard, or been extorted from them by stress of circumstances. They are in their generation wise enough to know how strong an impulse will be imparted to their destructive efforts by the dissensions of the Clergy, the mutual recriminations of different sets or classes of Clergymen and the consequent forfeiture, on the part of the whole body, of the confidence of the people, who are taught to suspect them of insincerity. These foes of the Church, having, by their arts of cajolery, prevailed upon those of the Clergy, whom they claim for friends but whom they cannot in their hearts respect, to revile and depreciate others of their Order, will rejoice in a perceptible approach towards the accomplishment of their main design ; and will look, with a sarcastic and disdainful smile, on the allies, whom they shall have rendered subservient to their purpose.

But, after all, what do such reflections as are noticed to have been cast upon the Clergy of the present or of preceding times really mean? To what do the oft-repeated insinuations or charges of insincerity and prevarication amount? Vague generalities, rhetorically set forth and adorned,

may impose upon careless readers or hearers.
Will any one in earnest say that he sincerely
believes Hooker and Sanderson and Barrow,
Beveridge and Pearson and Waterland (and, of
the host that might be named, how few are these!)
to have been inferior, in understanding and in
honesty, in just conception of the meaning of the
Articles, in ability to estimate the true import of
Subscription and in deference to the dictates of an
enlightened conscience—will any one seriously say
that he believes such men to have been, in
these respects, inferior to the wisest and the best
of his own contemporaries?

There is indeed some appearance of novelty of
argument, when attention is called to what is
represented to be a peculiar feature of the condition
of our affairs at present.

It is insisted, by the advocates of change, that
the Candidates for Holy Orders are far fewer
than they formerly were; and that, of those
who present themselves, a comparatively small
number belong to that class of " intelligent,
" thoughtful, highly educated young men[n]," from
which it was usual to receive them and from
which (as all must grant) it is desirable that the
ranks of our Ministry should be, from time to
time, replenished. Several causes are confessed

---

[n] Letter, &c. p. 30. And again, p. 63, in the application,
calculated rather to amuse than to convince, of a well-told
tale.

by the parties, thus representing the actual state of
things, to be at work in producing the result stated
and lamented. But the chief of the assignable
causes is said to be the difficulty of reconciling
many, whose " tastes, characters and gifts best
fit them°" for the Sacred Profession, to the prescribed condition of Subscription ; and the only
effectual remedy for an evil, supposed to threaten
disastrous consequences, is pronounced to be the
removal of this obstacle out of the way. It is
urged that, in order at once to relieve the minds
of the scrupulous and to supply the pressing wants
of the Church, access to the Ministerial Office
must be rendered perfectly free for all who desire
to enter upon it, by an abandonment of the
security, hitherto required, for each Candidate's
own sincere belief of the doctrines of the Church,
as they are stated in the Articles, and for his
consequent fidelity and zeal, in teaching and
enforcing those doctrines.

It is apprehended that the "remedy" would
prove " worse than the disease°."

Instances there probably are, although, it is to
be hoped, not so many as are sometimes supposed,
of youthful members of our Church, who pause
and hesitate on the threshold of the Ministry,
under the influence of doubts, with which they are
perplexed and of difficulties, by which they have

been harassed and are disturbed. Their state of painful suspense and of anxiety may be well imagined. It must be with the utmost reluctance that they meditate a total change of the plan of life, previously formed for them and by them. It cannot but be that with sincere and sad regret they now shrink from that dedication of themselves to God, whereby they had before humbly hoped to be " severed and sanctified to be employed in " His service, the highest advancement that mortal " creatures on earth can be raised unto ᵠ." In the mean time, they are to be honoured for an integrity, which refuses to accept the proffered aid of a miserable and misleading casuistry. They decline an outward compliance with that, which they do not inwardly approve. They give no heed to instructors, who undertake to shew them how they may employ the terms of " allowance,"— of " assent and consent,"—when those terms shall, by evasive wiles of interpretation, have been robbed of all their meaning. Having preserved an uncorrupted sense of right and wrong, they may be recalled from the mistakes, into which they have been betrayed by guides of opinion, to whom they first gave their affections and then surrendered their judgment. They may yet recover the satisfaction and peace of mind, of which they have deplored the loss. It may please God to reward their firm adherence to the course, which they at

ᵠ Eccles. Pol. v. 80, 6.

present discern to be that of duty, by imparting to them ampler and clearer views of duty and by strengthening them for a firm and diligent discharge of every duty so discovered. It is by no means impossible that, of their number, many may, after due inquiry and upon mature reflection, seek admission to Holy Orders and become " faithful dispensers of the Word of God and of " His holy Sacraments." Should the event, however, prove otherwise; should the Church miss the Ministerial services of all those, whom the condition of Subscription actually repels, there is no reason to fear that the evil will prove permanent. The noblest of all callings will soon re-assert its own dignity; and, in the clear light of a moral atmosphere, that shall be once more happily freed from the mists and exhalations of a now-prevailing scepticism, will shine forth with a lustre, sure in future, as heretofore, to attract the regards and win the love of aspirants after " the " honour that cometh from God only." A temporary inconvenience may be suffered; but will itself admit of being alleviated and gradually removed by the vigilance and prudence of our Spiritual Rulers, who will not be forgetful of the principle prescribed for their choice of Candidates by a grave authority: " I cannot see what " one duty there is, which always ought to go " before Ordination, but only care of the party's " worthiness, as well for integrity and virtue as

" knowledge—yea, for virtue more, inasmuch as
" defect of knowledge may sundry ways be
" supplied[r]."

If, in acting on this principle, the Bishops of
our Church are for a while at a loss for so copious
and so varied a supply of Candidates as they desire,
they will search after and will be sure to find,
in sufficient number for the places to be filled,
possessors of the indispensable qualifications of
good sense, sound judgment and fervent piety,
together with competent information on subjects
both sacred and secular. At all events, it is by
no means clear to a mind, accustomed to the
ordinary processes of thought and argument, that
the situation of affairs, in respect of a real or
supposed lack of Candidates for Holy Orders,
furnishes any sound or valid reason for relaxing,
much less for abandoning, the test of Subscription. On the supposition of the most strenuous
advocates of such relaxation or abandonment,
the parties, in whose behalf they plead, are for
the present disqualified alike for satisfactorily
undertaking and for successfully discharging
Ministerial duties. They have as yet formed no
fixed opinions. They entertain no settled views.
Learners themselves on all subjects open to dis-
cussion, they dare not teach any definite lessons.
Uncertain what to think and what to do, they
wisely refrain from attempting to guide others.

[r] Eccles. Pol. v. 80. 13.

Although they are entitled to be treated with the utmost forbearance and tenderness, in the prospect of their ultimate relief from the suspense of indecision, still they now are and, as long as their suspense shall last, will continue to be in a condition of mind totally unfit for entrance on the Sacred Profession. The barrier of Subscription excludes them from the inclosure of the Ministry. They are of the number of persons, whom that barrier was raised and is kept standing on purpose to exclude. Happily for themselves and for the Church, it avails to effect its intended purpose in their instance. And shall it therefore be removed? As well may the owner of fertile lands, reclaimed from the sea, listen to advisers, bidding him clear away the mounds and fences, against which the waves have long dashed in vain, as the Church lend a willing ear to counsellors, who entice her, by getting rid of Subscription, to open the flood-gates to an overwhelming tide that would immediately rush in, with its two currents, at first sight and apparently counteracting but really co-operating with each other—those, namely, of Negative Religion, Neology and Infidelity, on the one side, and of Romanism, on the other.

The truth is that the Reformed Church of England has, from the first, lain and still lies under an obligation, which cannot be either escaped or evaded, to exact from every one of those, whom she admits into the ranks of her Ministry, an assurance, as strong as language can make it, of the agreement of his own individual opinions, views and sentiments with her distinctive Confession of Faith. If indeed that distinctive Confession were (as it has lately been described to be*) " a mass of " heterogeneous Tudor dogmas, which no human " being can believe to be even self-consistent, much " less to be absolute and final truth;" or, if the same Confession were justly liable to the censure, which, in somewhat milder terms, has been passed upon it‘, " as, on its very face, repelling the notion " of Subscriptions, such as are *now* required by " law",'' and as " full of acknowledged imper- " fections;" it would become the Church to look well to the affair and to devise, without delay, expedients of alteration and amendment. Widely different is the estimate of the nature and value of the Thirty-nine Articles, which has been usually formed and is believed even now to prevail

* By Goldwin Smith, M.A. and Regius Professor of Modern History in the University of Oxford, in one of his Letters to the Editor of the Daily News.

‘ By Dr. Stanley, in his Letter to the Bishop of London, page 12.

" From the introduction of the word " *now*" into this clause, one would suppose that allusion is made to some change of the law or of the terms of Subscription, which has rendered Subscriptions of the present day different from Subscriptions of former times. What is that change? When was it effected?

generally. The writer last quoted must be supposed
to have shut his eyes to what he calls " the light
" of the able Commentary of Hey[x]," before he
expressed himself as he has done respecting the
Articles, and the men who drew them up ; for
Professor Hey informs his readers, that " the
" persons, who compiled our Articles, were men of
" the first *ability*. As scholars, we are mere children
" to them. The Scriptures they were conversant in
" to a degree, of which few now have any conception
" (so, at least, I believe). Ecclesiastical history,
" of facts and opinions, lay open before them ; yet
" they were not mere scholars, nor monks, nor
" monkish men, but skilled in government, knowing
" men and manners, liberal in behaviour, free
" from all fanaticism, full of probity, yet guided in
" their measures by prudence." " No set of men
" could be chosen, nor any circumstances, more
" *likely* to form a good set of Articles. They would
" fall short of nothing attainable, through indolence
" or cowardice. They would set nothing down
" carelessly, on the presumption of its passing
" unexamined. They would overshoot nothing,
" in hopes of catching a few. They had nothing
" for it but to fix on that, which right reason and
" good feelings would embrace." " If it be asked,
" why men do not commonly *esteem* our Articles
" according to this account? I would answer: really
" the chief thing, which hinders us from esteeming

" them, is our own *ignorance.*—We proceed in a
" petulant manner, reasoning superficially and
" despising what we ought to venerate. Let us
" then first suspect ourselves ; and then, after
" examination of ourselves, we may freely try" the
compilers of the Articles. " It frequently happens
" that we find fault with others, (especially if they
" are plain and unassuming) when the fault is
" only in ourselves ʸ." Be this however as it may ;
be the estimate, which Professor Hey formed and
forcibly expressed, of " the *worth* or *value*" of our
existing Articles, right or wrong; one thing is
certain : the Church of England must have a
distinctive Confession. The exigency of circumstances, which compelled our Reformers to frame
Articles of Religion, was not different in kind, was
scarcely different in degree, from the exigency,
which compels their successors and representatives
of the present day to keep up and maintain a body
of Articles, that are to serve for a bond of union
and concord among the members of the Church
within, and for an effectual means of distin-
guishing them from those that are without.

It is in the twofold character, of a branch of
the Church Catholic and of an Established or
National Church, that the Church of England
must have, and having must employ and use, for
her vindication and security, her own *distinctive*

ʸ Lectures in Divinity, book iv.—Introduction, sect. 3. pp.
204, 205, and 206 of vol. ii.

Confession, whatever that may be—whether it be
her present Confession, or some modification of
that Confession, or some substitute for it.

In the first place, the Church of England, as a
Branch of the Church Catholic, is bound to ascertain beforehand that all those, whose Ministerial
services she is about to accept, are prepared to
preserve inviolate and to hand on unimpaired that
very deposit of truth, either gathered and inferred
from Holy Scripture, or consistent therewith, which
has been entrusted to her charge and custody.
And how can she acquit herself of this obligation,
save by subjecting her Candidates for Holy Orders
to the test of such a Subscription as must, by
reason of the terms in which it is expressed, imply
their cordial acceptance of her doctrinal statements
and their own agreement of opinion and view with
those statements? The Protestants of the Con-
tinent, the Presbyterians of Scotland and the
Separatists of all classes and sorts amongst ourselves,
have, by the necessity of the case, been led to
adopt similar or analogous measures, which, in
some instances, they still retain. And well may
it here be asked; What have " Geneva and the
" Swiss Cantons, and some Protestant States of
" Germany, and the French Protestant Church,"
gained by the "gradual extinction or modification"
of their original Subscriptions[1]? What encourage-
ment does their experience give to a trial of the

[1] Letter, &c. p. 37.

plan, recommended to ourselves, of letting "the "National Confessions remain as acknowledged "and venerated standards of doctrine, while Or- "dained Ministers merely engage to teach their "flocks faithfully out of the Word of God ?" In the countries and regions, to which reference is here made, the "standards of doctrine" are, it is to be feared, retained merely as objects of anti- quarian interest and of occasional curiosity and research. The "Ordained Ministers" are neither guided and directed by those *nominally* "venerated "standards" in their teaching, nor admonished and reproved for real or suspected errors by any legal or even moral reference to the same standards. But the instance of the Church of Rome is, with an air of triumph, alleged to justify the proposed abandonment of Subscription : "From the Clergy "of the Roman Catholic Church no Subscription "is required at all ; nor, at their Ordination, any "declaration of belief*."

The latter part of this statement is not perfectly accurate. Before the ceremonies of Ordination to the *Priesthood* in the Church of Rome are finished, although not until after the Sacerdotal Order is by some Ritualists considered to have been con- ferred, the "*Ordained Priests*" (*Sacerdotes Ordinati*) are required to recite the Apostles' Creed, as the profession of that Faith, "*quam prœdicaturi sunt.*" It may therefore be said of them that, "*at* their

* Letter, &c. p. 36, note.

"Ordination, they make a declaration of belief;"
and it is worthy of special notice that they do
this in such form of the Primitive Creed as bears
striking witness against the innovations and cor-
ruptions of Rome, introduced into the Creed of
Pius IV. Notwithstanding however a slight in-
accuracy of statement, the general assertion may
be allowed that, *before* Ordination, the Romish
Clergy are not required to make Subscriptions
or Declarations corresponding with those which
are prescribed by our own Church. It may be
farther conceded that from the Romish Offices of
Ordination is absent all but a faint trace of those
Questions and Answers, which occur in our Forms
of the Ordering of Deacons and of Priests. The
example of Rome therefore may be alleged in
favour of banishing from our Offices these charac-
teristic features, which have arrested the attention
of almost all observers and have often called forth,
from eye-witnesses of our Ceremonies and from
commentators on our Forms, strong expressions
of approval and even of admiration. As Rome
does without them, so, it will be said, may we.
And, after all, but slight account seems to be
made of them, as securities remaining after the
surrender of Subscription.

"Candidates for Orders would still stumble
"at them. No doubt some would[b]." As little
can it be doubted that a restless agitation for their

[b] Letter, &c. p. 57.

removal would soon begin and incessantly go on ; and of the inconvenience of such agitation it will not be thought worth while to incur the risk by those who are of opinion that, of the Questions and Answers the most stringent (in some import- ant respects) of the whole number " probably " would not exclude a Roman Catholic or a " Greek," or are " such as most reasonable " Christians would at once accept[e]."

When, however, we are thus invited to con- template the case of the Church of Rome and are allured to imitate her example of management in " preserving unity, without the help of preliminary " promises or oaths[d]," on the part of her Can- didates for Orders or her Clergy, the feeling awakened can scarcely be any other than one of unfeigned surprise. Is the fact overlooked or forgotten that the Church of Rome has her own method of striving to accomplish that end of unity, at which we also aim ; and therefore stands in no need of the Subscriptions and stipu- lations, the vows and promises, to which the Church of England has recourse ? Her discipline of Sacramental Confession is the powerful instru- ment, by which she renders impossible the least outward departure from her system, whether of doctrine or of practice ; and by which she effec- tually hinders the putting forth of one word, oral or written, of dissent from her enlarged and

adulterated Creed, or of so much as a doubt
respecting a single particle of that Creed. Her
Candidates for Orders, being for the most part
(indeed with rare exceptions) destined for the
Sacred Profession from a tender age, are trained
in Seminaries and Colleges expressly set apart for
their use and reserved for them alone. They are
subject, from their earliest years, to the law, which
prescribes Confession to every youth " *eo tempore,*
" *cum inter bonum et malum discernendi vim*
" *habet, in ejusque mentem dolus cadere potest*[e]."
Accustomed to the restraint, thus from the first
applied, the Candidate for Orders takes each of
the several successive steps towards the lowest of
the three Sacred Orders, as well as each following
step of advance to the Priesthood, under the
condition of *previous Confession.* The rule of the
Tridentine Catechism on the subject is sufficiently
clear and explicit. It is as follows: " *cum Sacra-*
" *menta percipimus, toties Confessio prætermittenda*
" *non est*[f]." But, not content with this general
regulation, the Church of Rome takes care that,
in express terms, upon every Candidate be en-
joined " *prævia Confessio,*" as among the necessary
preliminaries, on every one of the separate occasions, which, beginning with the *Tonsure,* end in
admission to the *Sacerdotal Order.* And so is
fully justified the statement of the Catechism:

[e] Cat. Trid. ii. De Pœn. Sac. s. 58.
[f] Cat. Trid. ii. De Pœn. Sac. s. 59.

" Sanctam illam consuetudinem in Ecclesia servari
" animadvertimus ut qui Sacris initiandi sunt, prius
" Pœnitentiæ Sacramento conscientiam purgare
" diligenter studeant [s]*."*

A Church, which in the case of those, whom
she rears for her Ministry, thus crushes thought
from the first dawn of reason and forbids inquiry
by excluding it, may be expected to produce and
is, in fact, found to produce a fair external show
of unity amongst her Clergy.

There is, however, a far better chance of secur-
ing the advantage of such unity of purpose, sen-
timent and action as is alone attainable in a
numerous society and alone valuable, when a
Church requires (as our own Church does) from
her Candidates for Orders assent to Articles,
previously submitted to their careful examination,
and encourages afterwards, on the part of her
Ordained Ministers, a full and free investigation of
the subject-matter of those very Articles—an
investigation, to be begun and carried on in a
spirit of confiding reliance on the truth, already
ascertained and accepted, but admitting of being
illustrated and confirmed.

In the second place, the Church of England, as
an Established or National Church, lies under a
solemn obligation to employ, as she has heretofore
employed, her *distinctive* Confession. She has no
right to claim or to enjoy the favour and protection

[s] Cat. Trid. ii. De Ord. Sac. s. 55.

of the State, unless she can answer for her Clergy that their moral and religious teaching shall be positive and definite; and unless she can engage that their influence, so far as it flows from and depends on station and endowment, shall be exercised for the public good, according to a thoroughly understood and universally approved system of doctrine and duty. And how is it possible for the Church thus to answer—how is it possible for the Church to enter into or to fulfil such an engagement—unless she carefully explores and satisfactorily ascertains, not only the moral, intellectual and literary qualifications of her Candidates for Holy Orders, but also the agreement of their views and opinions with her recognised standards of faith and practice? If the precautions hitherto taken with a view to this momentous end (of which Subscription to the Articles is among the chief) are once abandoned, without the substitution for them of any equivalent measures, the Church of England will speedily forfeit, as she will have deserved to forfeit, all title to the privileges and possessions of an Established Church. Is this then the result really contemplated by those, who loudly call for the entire " removal of Sub- " scriptions?" Are they willing to imperil that Institution of their native land, with which the Monarchy of England and all the precious rights and liberties of Englishmen are indissolubly linked and inseparably associated? Excellently did the late Bishop Blomfield say in the House of Lords, on one of the many occasions of Debate, on which he distinguished himself: " The party, " bent upon destruction, know perfectly well that, " through the medium of the Church, the Mon- " archy may be most successfully assailed; for, " if the Church falls, all the other happy and " glorious Institutions of the country will follow. " If ever the Church should be cast down, it " will involve the Throne in its ruin[h]." But on this second branch of the subject—on the indispensable necessity to an Established Church of a *distinctive* Confession of Faith, to be subscribed by all its Ministers—the following words of wisdom, uttered by Mr. Burke, in the memorable Debate on the Feathers' Tavern Petition, deserve to be well weighed :

" It ill becomes your gravity," (so he is by himself recorded to have said to the House of Commons) " on the Petition of a few Gentlemen, to listen to any " thing that tends to shake one of the capital pillars " of the State and alarm the body of your people." " These Gentlemen" (the Petitioners) " complain " of hardships. They want to be preferred Clergy- " men in the Church of England, as by law " established; but their consciences will not suffer " them to conform to the doctrines and practices " of that Church; that is, they want to be teachers " in a Church, to which they do not belong; and

[h] Memoir of Bishop Blomfield, vol. i. p. 266.

" it is an odd sort of hardship. They want to
" receive the emoluments, appropriated for teach-
" ing one set of doctrines, whilst they are teaching
" another. A Church, in any legal sense, is only
" a certain system of religious doctrines and prac-
" tices, fixed and ascertained by some law; and
" the Establishment is a tax laid by the Sovereign
" authority for payment of those, who so teach
" and practise. For no Legislature was ever so
" absurd as to tax its people to support men for
" teaching and acting as they please, but by some
" prescribed rule. The hardship amounts to this—
" that the people of England are not taxed to pay
" the Clergy for teaching as Divine truths their
" own particular fancies. By way of relieving
" these Gentlemen" (the Petitioners) " it would be
" a cruel hardship on the people to be compelled
" to pay men to condemn, as heretical, the doc-
" trines, which the people repute to be orthodox;
" and to reprobate, as superstitious, the practices,
" which the people use as pious and holy.

" The matter does not concern toleration, but
" establishment; and it is not the rights of private
" conscience that are in question, but the propriety
" of the terms, which are proposed by law as a title
" to public emoluments; so that the complaint is
" not that there is not toleration of diversity in opi-
" nion, but that diversity of opinion is not rewarded
" by Bishoprics, Rectories and Collegiate Stalls.
" When Gentlemen complain of the Subscription

" as matter of grievance, the complaint arises from
" confounding private judgment, whose rights are
" anterior to law, and the qualifications which the
" law creates for its own Magistracies, whether
" civil or religious.

" If you will have Religion publicly practised and
" publicly taught, you must have a power to say
" what that Religion will be, which you will pro-
" tect and encourage ; and to distinguish it by
" such marks and characteristics as you, in your
" wisdom, shall think fit. Your determination
" may be unwise in this as in other matters ; but
" it cannot be unjust, hard, or oppressive, or
" contrary to the liberty of any man, or in the
" least degree exceeding your province.

" That, of which the Petitioners complain, is
" therefore as a grievance fairly none at all;
" nothing but what is essential not only to the
" order, but to the liberty of the whole community.

" The Petitioners are so sensible of the force of
" these arguments that they do admit of one Sub-
" scription, that is, to the Scripture.

" The Subscription to Scripture is the most
" astonishing idea I ever heard and will amount
" to just nothing at all. To ascertain Scripture,
" you must have one Article more, and you must
" define what that Scripture is, which you mean
" to teach. There are, I believe, very few, who,
" when Scripture is so ascertained, do not see the
" absolute necessity of knowing what general

" doctrine a man draws from it, before he is sent
" down authorized by the State to teach it as
" pure doctrine.

" If we do not get some security for the doctrine,
" which a man draws from Scripture, we not only
" permit, but we actually pay for, all the dangerous
" fanaticism, which can be produced to corrupt
" our people and to derange the public worship of
" the country[i]."

Twenty years after the delivery of the Speech,
from which the above-cited passages are taken,
the great Statesman and Orator, in a Letter to Sir
Hercules Langrishe, M.P.[k] shewed that his views
remained unaltered :

" Our predecessors in legislation were not so
" irrational (not to say impious) as to form an
" operose Ecclesiastical Establishment, and even
" to render the State itself in some degree sub-
" servient to it, when their Religion (if such it
" might be called) was nothing but a mere *negation*
" of some other, without any positive idea either of
" doctrine, discipline, worship, or morals, in the
" scheme which they professed themselves and which
" they imposed upon others, even under penalties and
" incapacities. No! No! This never could have
" been done even by reasonable Atheists? They
" who think Religion of no importance to the
" State, have abandoned it to the conscience or

[i] Works of Edmund Burke, vol. x. p. 10—21.

[k] Works of Edmund Burke, vol. vi. p. 316—318.

" caprice of the individual. They make no provision
" for it whatsoever ; but leave every club to make
" or not a voluntary contribution towards its sup-
" port, according to their fancies. This would be
" consistent. The other always appeared to me to
" be a monster of contradiction and absurdity.
" It was for that reason that, some years ago,
" I strenuously opposed the Clergy, who petitioned,
" to the number of about three hundred, to be
" freed from the Subscription to the Thirty-nine
" Articles, without proposing to substitute any
" other in their place.

" There never has been a Religion of the State
" (the few years of the Parliament only excepted)
" but that of the *Episcopal Church of England;*
" the Episcopal Church of England, before the
" Reformation, connected with the See of Rome ;
" since then, disconnected and protesting against
" some of her doctrines, and against the whole of
" her authority, as binding in our National
" Church. Nor did the fundamental laws of this
" kingdom (in Ireland it has been the same) ever
" know, at any period, any other Church, as an
" object of Establishment; or, in that light, any
" other Protestant Religion.

" The Church of Scotland knows as little of
" Protestantism *undefined,* as the Churches of
" England and Ireland do. She has, by the
" Articles of Union, secured to herself the per-
" petual establishment of the Confession of Faith

" and the Presbyterian Church Government. In
" England, even in the troubled Interregnum, it
" was not thought fit to establish a *negative*
" Religion ; but the Parliament settled the Presby-
" terian, as the Church discipline ; the Directory,
" as the rule of worship ; and the Westminster
" Catechism, as the institute of faith.

" This is to shew that at no time was the
" Protestant Religion *undefined* established here
" or any where else, as I believe[1]."

As long as the considerations, thus powerfully
urged by one, whose writings deserve far more
attention than is bestowed upon them in the present
day, shall continue to have force (and who will
venture to say that any thing has occurred, in the
course of the years that have elapsed since they
were urged, or is likely hereafter to occur, to lessen
their force or limit their application ?) the *Established* Church of England will be bound to insist
on Subscription to the Thirty-nine Articles, or to
some similar Confession of Faith, as the indispensable condition of admission to her Ministry—
a Subscription, obliging each Subscriber not to
silence or *peace only*, but to a *serious belief* of that
to which he subscribes. This distinction between
two separate kinds of Subscription has been frequently made, and is universally understood. The
notion, however, that the Subscription of the
Candidates for Orders and of the Clergy of the

[1] Works of Edmund Burke, vol. vi. p. 316—318.

Church of England, in the terms by law prescribed, is no more than a Subscription to Articles of peace, has been seriously entertained by few and has been of late but seldom mentioned, except to be repudiated. It may seem hazardous to assert thus much, in opposition to the following statement:

" With regard to the Clerical Subscriptions, "many high authorities have declared that Sub- " scription to the Articles is simply an acknow- " ledgment of them as Articles of peace, not " to be impugned, but not of necessity to be " believed by the Subscriber. Such was the well- " known opinion of Archbishop Bramhall and " Bishop Bull and Mr. Burke, and, to a considerable " degree, of Bishop Burnet and Professor Hey, " and has, within our own memory, been forcibly " expressed both in public journals and by leading " Prelates[m]."

" The public journals and leading Prelates," here concerned, may be passed over in silence. Their names are not mentioned. No judgment can be formed of their authority. Archbishop Bramhall, Bishop Bull, and Mr. Burke, must be allowed to be high authorities on such a subject. Was then the opinion above stated " the well-known " opinion " of Archbishop Bramhall? Rather does it not appear to have been an opinion imputed to him, through a faulty inference from and a mis- application of his language? So says Bishop

[m] Letter, &c. p. 21.

Burnet, who, in speaking of the Articles as Articles of Church communion, or of peace only, for the Lay members of the Church, and in referring, it would seem, to the very passages of Archbishop Bramhall's "Schism Guarded," which have suggested the representation, remarks:

"The citations that are brought from those two "great Primates, Laud and Bramhall, go no "further than this: they do not seem to relate "to the Clergy that subscribe the Articles; but "to the Laity and body of the people. The "people, who do only join in communion with "us, may well continue to do so, though they "may not be fully satisfied with every proposition "in the Articles"."

Again it may be asked, Was the opinion, ascribed to Archbishop Bramhall, "the well-known "opinion" of Bishop Bull also? The latter case is in fact as doubtful as the former. The passage of Bishop Bull's "Vindication of the Church of "England," to which reference for his "well-"known opinion" is made, is far from being decisive in its evidence. On the contrary, the careful reader of the whole passage will perceive that it relates chiefly to the Laity and recognises a plain distinction between the assent or acquiescence of the Lay members of the Church and the Subscription of the Clergy, abundantly warranting the observation of Dr. Arnold:

▪ Introduction to Exposition of the Articles, p. 7:

"The expressed opinions of Bull and others"
on Subscription are "not at all to be taken to
"such an extent, as if the Articles were Articles
"of peace merely°."

Once more is it to be asked, Was this "the
"well-known opinion" of Mr. Burke? The extracts already given from a Speech and a Letter of
his are difficult to be reconciled with the supposition. It is however to be presumed that he
has somewhere expressed himself distinctly on the
subject of an important change of view, which
must have taken place subsequently to the date of
his Letter to Sir Hercules Langrishe. The eager
curiosity, which a marginal reference to "Speeches,
"I. 94." promises to gratify, is doomed to disappointment. The reference is too vague to be
of any use. It seems to be to the *First* of *Four*
Volumes of *a Collection of Speeches,* (not always to
be trusted for accuracy of Report) and to *page* 94
of that Volume. If at a loss to find any allusion to
the subject there, the inquirer has recourse to the
well-known Edition of the Works of Mr. Burke, in
Fourteen octavo volumes, he will discover in page 94
(the coincidence is remarkable) of Vol. iii., a passage
of a Speech, made on moving Resolutions for Con-
ciliation with the Colonies in 1775 (soon after the
Speech on the Feathers' Tavern Petition and long
before the date of the Letter to Sir Hercules

° Life of Dr. Arnold, vol. ii. p. 152.

Langrishe) in which mention does indeed occur of
"*Articles of Peace :*"

"I put my foot" (says the eloquent Debater)
"on the tracks of our forefathers, where I can
"neither wander nor stumble. Determining to
"fix Articles of Peace, I was resolved not to
"be wise beyond what was written ; I was resolved
"to use nothing else than the form of sound
"words ; to let others abound in their own sense ;
"and carefully to abstain from all expressions
"of my own." Does the illustration here bor-
rowed from a distinction of Articles, familiar
to every mind, convey the most distant hint
of the speaker's opinion of the import and meaning of Clerical Subscription to the Thirty-nine
Articles of the Church of England ? Where then
—in what passage of his numerous works—does
Mr. Burke so declare the opinion ascribed to him,
as to justify the statement that it was his "well-
"known opinion ?" Until a plain answer is returned
to this question, they surely may be excused,
who choose to gather Mr. Burke's sentiments on
Subscription from his own, as yet unrefuted,
reasonings and from his corresponding conduct.

In the instances of Bishop Burnet and Professor
Hey, a qualifying phrase is employed. It is only
"to a considerable degree" that the Bishop and
the Professor are stated to have shared "the
"well-known opinion" of Archbishop Bramhall,
Bishop Bull and Mr. Burke.

The " well-known," because explicitly declared,
" opinion of Bishop Burnet" was in favour of
abandoning Subscription to the Thirty-nine
Articles altogether and so " leaving men to" what
he considered " the due freedom of their
" thoughts." But in what sense he understood
the required Subscription of the Clergy, as it
existed in his day and as it still exists in ours—
what was "the considerable degree," to which
he entertained the view assigned to him—every
reader of the Introduction to his Exposition of
the Articles may for himself judge.

" I come in the next place " (says the honest
Prelate[p]) " to consider what the Clergy are bound
" to by their Subscriptions. The meaning of
" every Subscription is to be taken from the
" design of the imposer and from the words
" of the Subscription itself. The title of the
" Articles bears that they were agreed upon
" in Convocation, '*for the avoiding of diversities*
" *of opinions, and for the stablishing consent*
" *touching true Religion;*' where it is evident that *a*
" *consent in opinion* is designed. The thirty-sixth
" Canon is express for the Clergy, requiring them to
" subscribe *willingly* and *ex animo,* and *acknow-*
" *ledge all and every Article to be agreeable to the*
" *Word of God:* upon which Canon it is that the
" Form of Subscription runs in these words, which
" seem expressly to declare a man's own opinion,

p Introduction to Exposition of Articles, p. 9.

" and not a bare consent to an Article of peace, or
" an engagement to silence and submission. The
" Statute of the 13th Eliz. c. 12., which gives the
" legal authority to our requiring Subscription in
" order to a man's being capable of a Benefice,
" requires that every Clergyman should read the
" Articles in the Church, with a declaration of his
" unfeigned assent to them. These things make
" it appear very plain that the Subscriptions of
" the Clergy must be considered as a declaration
" of their own opinion, and not as a bare obligation
" to silence." From the Royal Declaration, pre-
fixed to the Articles, " two things are to be
" inferred. The one is that the Subscription does
" import an assent to the Article. And the other
" is that, an Article being conceived in such
" general words that it can admit of different
" literal and grammatical senses, even when the
" senses given are plainly contrary one to another,
" yet both" (parties thus differently understanding
an Article) " may subscribe the Article with a
" good conscience and without any equivocation."

Will not the readers of these extracts be
inclined to think and say that Bishop Burnet,
applying himself deliberately and *ex professo* to
the consideration of the subject of Clerical Subscription, has in the strongest possible manner
disclaimed and disowned the opinion, which is
asserted to have been his " to a considerable
" degree?" Nor can it•be doubted that his

Exposition of the Articles (which, with all its deficiencies and faults, has been deservedly accounted an excellent and useful work) has mainly contributed towards settling men's minds in an opinion of Subscription, directly contrary to that, which he himself is injuriously charged with having held.

The Divinity Lectures of Professor Hey are by no means destitute of value. The proficient in Theology, already well informed and of mature judgment, may advantageously avail himself of them in various ways. But for a youthful student, who is desirous of understanding the meaning of the Articles, in order that he may afterwards, with ease of mind and satisfaction, in the capacity of a Candidate for Orders, subscribe to them, scarcely any thing could be more unfortunate than to be placed under that Author's guidance. A student so circumstanced, looking for light, would grope in darkness. Seeking relief from doubt, suspense and uncertainty, he would be in perpetual danger of becoming puzzled and perplexed. Professor Hey himself, however, has not gone so far as to avow the opinion on Subscription, which is stated to have been, at all events, " to a " considerable degree," held by him. His subtle distinctions and refining explications do indeed leave in doubt the amount of meaning of the Articles that is to remain, after all his suggested processes shall have been applied. But still he contends for some final residuum of meaning and grants that the Subscription of Candidates for Orders and of the Clergy, binding on the conscience, implies each Subscriber's acknowledgment that his own opinions and views are in harmony with that residuum of meaning[q] : " When a law " is made and continues in force, it is to be " obeyed. If then a law exists, requiring assent " to certain doctrines or agreement in opinion, " we now inquire, whether a man's honest intention " to teach the doctrines faithfully will excuse his " want of believing them[r] :—we maintain that such " intention will *not* be sufficient, without such " *belief* as will remain, after all those liberties" (of interpretation, that is, which he had sanctioned) " have been taken."

Again : " While Articles of faith exist, any one, " who is lawfully called to assent to them, must, " in strictness of duty, not only determine to act " regularly, but to declare his real opinion."

It is however time to bring these observations and with them this Pamphlet to a close. Out of the chief purpose of the preceding pages, that, namely, of vindicating the existing law and practice of Clerical Subscription to the Articles, has arisen another,

[q] Divinity Lect. Book iii. ch. 13. ss. 4 and 7.

[r] This inquiry well suits Professor Hey. How few besides himself would think of the possibility of a man's honest intention to teach *faithfully* doctrines, which he does not believe !

subordinate and, as it were, supplemental, purpose of removing some few names, more or less distinguished, from the list, in which they seem to have been without due caution included, of maintainers or favourers of the utterly untenable position, that the Thirty-nine Articles, offered for Subscription to Candidates for Holy Orders and to the Clergy, in the terms prescribed by law, are meant to be regarded as Articles of peace, or can be so understood.